Contents

Get ready, get set, go!

Some people are very **active**. They walk everywhere and they run upstairs. They're always on the go.

Other people are less active. They go by car. They take the lift and not the stairs. They sit and watch TV.

Star tip

Why not get up, get out and get some **exercise**? It will give you an **energy** boost.

Do it!

What did your body do today? Make a list of everything you did. How active were you?

Quick quiz!

Who is being active here? Who is being **inactive**?

Good for the body!

When you run about, your **heart** and **lungs** work harder. You feel warm and your face goes red. You feel out of breath.

All this is good for your body!

Star tip

Try to be active every day. Active people live longer and are **healthier**, too.

Think about it!

How many activities can you think of that make you feel out of breath?

Do it!

How big are your lungs? Take a deep breath and blow bubbles through a straw into a glass of water. Ask an adult to time you. The longer you keep going, the bigger your lungs. Have a competition with a friend or someone in the family.

Bigger and stronger

You use your **muscles** to move your body.

Being active is good for them. Using your muscles makes them grow bigger and stronger. Your **bones** grow stronger, too.

Do it!

Try throwing a Frisbee. It can be tricky at first, but every time you practise, the muscles in your arms 'learn' to do it better.

Think about it!

Can you think of an activity that would use the muscles in your legs? Which other activities would use your arm muscles?

Pull it, push it, bend it, stretch it! When you're active, your body moves in many different ways.

Kicking a ball uses the muscles in your legs. Swimming uses all your muscles!

Outdoor games

Sometimes we feel grumpy or bored. This is a good time to get out and do something active.

It will cheer you up and make you feel better.

Exercise makes you feel better. A game of football is a lot of fun and stops you feeling cross or bored.

Which of these activities would you enjoy doing?

climbing a rope ladder

tobogganing

hopscotch

badminton

go-karting

playing baseball

Do it! Which are your favourite outdoor games? Draw a picture of your friends and yourself having fun. Can you make your drawing 'action packed'?

High, low or in-between?

Some things we do use up more energy than others.

Running fast makes you puff and feel hot. This kind of exercise is HIGH activity.

Walking fast is MEDIUM activity. You feel warmer and a little out of breath.

Watching TV is LOW activity. You don't warm up and your breathing doesn't change.

Do it!

Write down all the things you enjoy doing. By the side of each activity, write 'H' for things that use up a lot of energy, 'L' for those that do not and 'M' for the ones in-between.

Star tip

Do high-activity things each day. You will feel healthy and sleep well at night.

Think about it!

Are these activities are high, medium or low? Reading, swimming, dancing, cycling, playing on a slide, painting, sitting at the computer, playing with a skipping rope?

An hour a day

To keep healthy, we need to get some exercise every day.

Try to make your bones and muscles work hard for at least an hour. This makes them grow bigger and stronger.

You don't have to be sporty. Dancing is a great way to use your muscles and bones. It makes your heart and lungs work harder, too.

You don't have to do an hour of exercise all in one go. You can do it in little bits.

Helping Mum or Dad wash the car, playing a ball game with a friend and running around in the park could all count towards your hour of exercise.

Do it!

Lie on a long piece of white paper and ask a friend to draw around you. Cut out your body shape and draw on pictures of yourself doing your daily exercise.

Active at school

School is a great place to be active. As well as PE lessons, there's space to run around and play safely in the playground.

Being active in the playground at break and lunchtime makes a change from sitting still in class.

Star tip

Try something new at an after-school club. You may find you're good at it!

How many of these children are being very active in the playground?

Do it! Find out what games your parents and grandparents played when they were at school. Are there any games you don't know? If so, ask them to show you how to play them.

Free-time fun!

What do you do in your free time after school? Do you go swimming or to Brownies, Cubs or another club?

Do you play football or go to the park at weekends? There's plenty of time to be active in the holidays, too.

Why not fly a kite or play a ball game?

18

Think about it!

When you're on holiday, you may get the chance to try something new. Which of these activities would you like to try?

Pony-trekking, swimming, cycling, swingball, canoeing, skiing?

Do it!

Have an activity contest with some friends! Who can bounce a ball for more than 30 seconds? Who can **limbo** under a broom?

Time to rest

You are active at school
and at home all day long,
and you use up energy.

In the evening you get tired.
You slow down. . . your eyes get
heavy. . . soon you are fast asleep.

Do it!

Draw a clock face and divide it into six parts. Now draw pictures of six things — one in each part — that you do each day. Draw a picture of yourself asleep in the final part.

Star tip

After school, play outside with a friend. You will feel relaxed and it will help you to sleep well at night.

While you're asleep, your body rests. When you wake up, you feel more ready to be active in the day ahead.

Glossary

active moving around and doing things

bones the hard parts inside the body

energy the get-up-and-go, or power, to be active

exercise activity for the body

healthy fit and well

heart the part of your body that pumps blood around the body

inactive sitting or lying still and not moving about

limbo dance under a bar leaning backwards

lungs the parts of the body that help you to breathe

muscles the parts of the body that help you to move

Index

Notes
for parents and teachers

- Encourage your children to keep an activity diary for a week. Together, write down the number of hours spent being active. How does this compare to the recommendation on pages 14 and 15 that children should do an hour's moderate activity a day?

- Try to think up ways that you and your children could be more active. Together, plan a number of 10-minute activity sessions. Try to do two of them every day.

- Discuss how much you travel by car or bus – e.g. to and from school, a club or a relative's house. Work out how long these journeys are and how long they would take on foot.

- How do children in the class get to and from school? Conduct a survey to find out.
  OR
- Find out what activities the children in the class do out of school. Use the information to draw a pictogram. Which is the most popular kind of exercise?

- Using books or the Internet, show your children pictures of the human body. Show them the position of the heart and lungs, and discuss how these work. Ask them to take a deep breath in and out. Which parts of the body move?

- Using books or the Internet, show your children pictures of the muscles and bones. Ask them to feel the bones in a friend's hands, feet and back. Can they find any muscles?

- Discuss the effects of exercise on the heart. Ask the children to place an ear against a friend's chest and listen to the heartbeat. Do this again after exercise. Can they hear a difference?

- Muscles get fatter when we use them. Measure your children around the top of their arms when they are stretched out straight. Then measure them again when the arms are bent. Is there any difference?

- Challenge your children to plan a series of activities that exercise different muscles in the body. Don't forget the muscles in the face and ears!

- Do your children know any playground rhymes? Using books and the Internet, research playground rhymes and make a collection in a special book. What games can be played to the rhymes?

- Sportsmen and sportswomen are often in the news. Do your children have any sporting heroes? If so, try and find out more about them and how they became interested in their sports.

- Encourage your children to make a tape or CD of their favourite music. They could listen to it on their headphones while they skip, play with a ball or work out a new dance routine.

- Ask your children to think of words that describe how activity can make us feel – e.g. hot, puffed, happy, lively. Suggest your children draw a picture for each word.

- Make a crossword puzzle for your children, using words in the glossary.

Exercise

Claire Llewellyn

QED Publishing

A catalogue record for this book is available from the British Library.

ISBN 1 84538 473 3

Written by Claire Llewellyn
Designed by Susi Martin
Editor Louisa Somerville
Consultant Ruth Miller B.Sc., M.I.Biol., C.Biol.
Illustrations John Haslam
Photographs Michael Wicks

Publisher Steve Evans
Editorial Director Jean Coppendale
Art Director Zeta Davies

Printed and bound in China

Picture credits

Key: t = top, b = bottom, c = centre, l = left, r = right, FC = front cover

Corbis Warren Morgan 9,/ Tim Pannell 10.
Gettyimages Altrendo images 7,/ David Rosenburg 8,/ David Madison 16.

Words in **bold** are explained

in the glossary on page 22.